CRUNCH, MUNCH, LUNCH!

TABLE OF CONTENTS

CRUNCH, MUNCH, LUNCH!

The Further Adventures of Humpty Dumpty

Humpty Dumpty, King of the Eggs,
Ran down the road on his little short legs.
After him, quickly, came forty-two cooks
Who lived in a castle of cookery books,
Charging and barging the length of the street,
Holding their eggbeaters ready to beat,
Shouting out *Omelettes!* and *Scrambled!* as well.
What a terrible shock for a king in a shell!
— *Margaret Mahy*

Lunchtime

Get up, get up, you lazy heads,
Get up, you lazy bunch.
We need those sheets for tablecloths,
It's nearly time for lunch!

– Anonymous

What did the sick banana tell its mother?
I don't peel good.

Dressing for Dinner

There was a young man named Joe Wall,
Who went to a fancy dress ball.
He went, just for fun,
Dressed up as a bun,
And a dog ate him up in the hall.

– Anonymous

Kilkenny Cats

There once were two cats of Kilkenny,
Each thought there was one cat too many.
So they fought and they howled,
And they scratched and they growled,
Till excepting their nails and the tips of their tails,
Instead of two cats, there weren't any.

– Anonymous

JOKE

Why did the cat work at the hospital?
It wanted to be a first-aid kit.

Plain Speaking

Cats don't need words
to speak.
Cats talk
with their tails
switch, switch,
or their ears
twitch, twitch,
or their walk
stalk-stalk.

A cat can move with
elegance and grace
from here to that place
while proudly proclaiming
in one superior
stare –
    I need
        only
            me!
            – Patricia Irene Johnson

Summer Dress

I found a nest today –
(no one at home
the birds had flown) –
all neatly lined with moss
and something more,
offcuts and threads galore
of dresses Mom had
made me in the spring.
There in a ring
of colors bright and gay,
woven among the moss
and twigs and grass
my summer dresses lay.

A pretty nest, I thought,
in which to rest.

– *Patricia Irene Johnson*

Observation

For the birds
there are no boundaries
to flight;
no one-way streets
or stops compulsory
or scarlet lights
to bring them to a halt,
unwilling and abrupt.
In fact, no obligations to
the other feathered
users of the sky.

For the birds
there is a boundlessness
of blue –
of unplumbed depths
where sparrows dash
in little urgent swoops,
and seagulls soar
on lazy silvered wings.
For the birds
there is the endlessness
of space.

– Patricia Irene Johnson

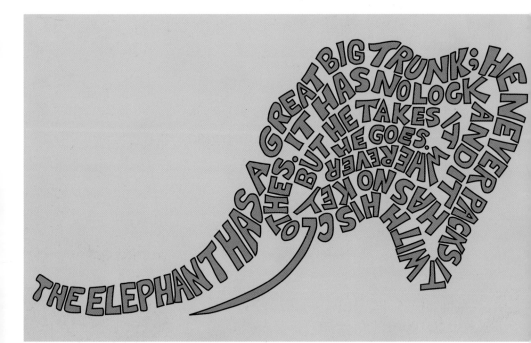

THE ELEPHANT HAS A GREAT BIG TRUNK; HE NEVER PACKS IT WITH HIS CLOTHES; IT HAS NO LOCK AND IT HAS NO KEY, BUT HE TAKES IT WHEREVER HE GOES.

JUST MY LUCK TO BE A DUCK

DON'T YOU WISH YOU WERE A FISH

JOKE

Why did the elephant change his sock
on the golf course?
Because he had a hole in one.

AN ELEPHANT HAS A LONG NOSE, A MONKEY HAS A LONG TAIL, A SNAIL IS ONLY LITTLE, BUT HE LEAVES A LONG, LONG TRAIL.

Little Miss Tucket

Little Miss Tucket
Sat on a bucket
Eating some peaches and cream;
And when a grasshopper
Tried hard to stop her,
She said, "Go away, or I'll scream!"
— *Anonymous*

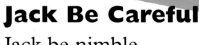

Jack Be Careful

Jack be nimble
Jack be quick
Silly Jack ate
A candlestick
And every time
He blew his nose
Flames shot out
And burnt his toes.
— *Tracey Shilling*

Mother Goose Rock and Roll

Old King Cole is a merry old soul.
He likes to dance to rock and roll.
On his big guitar he strums,
While Old Queen Cole plays on the drums.

And the fiddlers, in surprise,
Scratch their heads and blink their eyes.
Then they start dancing, 'cause fiddlers' feet
Can't help rocking to the King Cole beat.

– Margaret Mahy

JOKE

Which side of a lamb has the most wool?
The outside.

Who Has Seen the Wind?

Who has seen the wind?
> Neither I nor you,
But when the leaves hang trembling,
> The wind is passing through.

Who has seen the wind?
> Neither you nor I,
But when the trees bow down their heads,
> The wind is passing by.
> – *Christina Rossetti*

JOKE

What kind of dogs taste best in winter?
Chilly dogs.

A Rainy Day

I met a worm along my way.
You see, it was a rainy day.
Like me, he had a coat and hat,
And rubber boots, though long and flat.
And just like me, he splashed and played,
Writhed and wriggled, dug in clay.
And just like me, he stomped around,
Splashing mud, some up, some down.
But unlike me
(I was off to school, you see)
His teacher didn't frown.
> – *David Nuss*

Seasons

Spring is flowery, showery, bowery.
Summer is hoppy, croppy, poppy.
Autumn is slippy, drippy, nippy.
Winter is wheezy, sneezy, freezy.
> – *Mother Goose*

Rabbit's Ears

Our rabbit's ears will tell the time.
I don't know if she means it.
Her black ear's pointed down to *five*,
Every time she cleans it.

Her white ear proudly stands at *twelve*.
She doesn't tick or tock.
She's got no numbers, got no hands,
But says it's *five o'clock*.

Her ears stand straight for *midnight*,
But if she wonders who
Has moved a twig or kicked a stone,
Her ears say, *ten to two*.

– *Margaret Mahy*

Rhymes All the Time

I wish that I had enough time
To say all I say, but in rhyme.
I would like when I speak
To obtain what I seek
And make time to rhyme every line.

– *David Nuss*

JOKE

What kind of dog always arrives on time?
A watchdog.

"Tell me, Jason..."

"Yes, Noleen?"

"...Are we snakes that PRESS and CRUSH our victims till their bones CRACK, and the last breath is S-Q-U-E-E-Z-E-D out? Or are we snakes that have a poisonous BITE that kills our victims in a minute or two?"

"We PRESS and CRUSH our victims, Noleen."

"Thank goodness for that! I just bit my lip!"

JOKE

What does a polite snake say when it bites you?
Fangs a lot!